REBEL GIRLS ROCK

25 TALES OF WOMEN IN MUSIC

T0015158

Good Night Stories for Rebel Girls and Rebel Girls are registered trademarks. *Good Night Stories for Rebel Girls* and all other Rebel Girls titles are available for bulk purchase for sale promotions, premiums, fundraising, and educational needs. For details, write to sales@rebelgirls.com.

This is a work of creative nonfiction. It is a collection of heartwarming and thought-provoking stories inspired by the lives and adventures of 33 influential women and girls. It is not an encyclopedic account of the events and accomplishments of their lives.

www.rebelgirls.com

Some of the artwork in this book has been previously published in the books *Good Night Stories for Rebel Girls, Good Night Stories for Rebel Girls 2, Good Night Stories for Rebel Girls: 100 Immigrant Women Who Changed the World, Good Night Stories for Rebel Girls: 100 Real-Life Tales of Black Girl Magic, Good Night Stories for Rebel Girls: 100 Inspiring Young Changemakers,* and *Rebel Girls Lead.*

Library of Congress Control Number: 2022948130
Rebel Girls, Inc.
421 Elm Ave.
Larkspur, CA 94939

Text by Harriet Webster, Jess Harriton, Sarah Glenn Marsh, Sydnee Monday
Foreword by Joan Jett
Art direction by Giulia Flamini
Cover illustrations by Annalisa Ventura
Graphic design by Kristen Brittain
Special thanks: Carianne Brinkman, Eliza Kirby, Grace Srinivasiah, Jenny Marsh, Jes Wolfe, Marina Asenjo, Sarah Parvis

Printed in Italy
10 9 8 7 6 5 4 3 2 1
ISBN: 978-1-953424-44-0

CONTENTS

INTRODUCTION

Dear Rebels,

I must have been 10 or 11 when I started noticing rock and roll being played on the radio. Pop stars of the time like Donny Osmond weren't doing it anymore for my young ears. I was transfixed on rhythm-guitar-centered songs, like "All Right Now" by Free, or "Bang a Gong" by T. Rex. I wanted to make those sounds!

For Christmas a year or two later, I asked for an electric guitar. I thought there was no way my parents would buy it for me. But they did. Can you imagine? This was the early '70s, and little girls were not jamming on electric guitars. You might see a woman with an acoustic guitar sing folk music. That wasn't what I wanted. I wanted to form an all-girl band and make rock and roll. I wanted to play guitar loud and express everything I was thinking and feeling through the music. I wasn't going to hold back just because people thought girls shouldn't play guitar.

So, when I was a teenager, I formed a band with drummer Sandy West. We figured if we wanted to form an all-girl rock band, there had to be other girls who wanted the same thing! We set out to find them and formed The Runaways. Some people weren't supportive, but we loved playing and were not going to let anyone tell us what we could and could not do.

After the band broke up, I was heartbroken, but I formed a new band, and we were Joan Jett and the Blackhearts. I couldn't get a record deal and received more than 20 rejection letters. I started selling records at my shows from the trunk of my producer's Cadillac, and my indie label Blackheart was born. Blackheart is one of the longest-running indie labels and one of the first female-artist-owned labels.

Over the years, things have changed, but there are still people out there who believe girls shouldn't do everything that boys can do.

We need to change that by teaching kids not to treat one another differently based on gender and making sure there are plenty of women in positions of power.

It's one of the reasons I love this book—the stories show many of the ways women can shape the music business, as performers, instrumentalists, songwriters, producers, DJs, and on the business side too. As you flip through these pages, you will read about Joni Mitchell, whose honest, heartfelt lyrics were game-changing. There's Lizzo, who spreads a message of pride and empowerment for girls and brought the flute into pop music, and there's Fea, a Chicana riot grrrl punk band so fun and fearless, I signed them to my own label. All the women featured in this book have made an impact beyond the music industry—they've inspired people from all walks of life.

When I was five years old, my parents told me I could be anything I wanted to be—and I believed them. I hope you have someone in your life who is telling you that too. And, if not, let me be that person for you right now: you can be who and what you want to be in this world. Dream big, always. You want to be an astronaut or a chef or an archaeologist? Go for it. You want to make jazz or hip-hop or rock and roll? Go for it. Pick up the guitar or the flute or the cello or whatever helps you to express yourself and feel alive, and go for it. Play your heart out.

—Joan Jett

SCAN TO HEAR MORE!

BONUS! AUDIO STORIES!

Download the Rebel Girls app to hear longer stories about some of the unstoppable musicians in this book. You will also unlock creative activities and discover stories of other trailblazing women. Whenever you come across a bookmark icon, just scan the code, and you'll be whisked away on an audio adventure.

BIG MAMA THORNTON

BLUES SINGER

On a chilly day in Alabama, while families decorated Christmas trees and sang carols, a big present to the world named Willie Mae was born.

As they grew up, Willie and her brothers and sisters would sit in church pews every Sunday and listen to their father preach. Willie's favorite part was the music. Her mother's singing voice soothed her. As she watched the choir ladies sway to the songs, Willie tried to listen for only her mother's voice.

When Willie was just 14, her mother died. But the inspiration Willie found in her sweet voice never left her. Willie decided to chase her dream of becoming a blues singer.

She joined a music group in Georgia and traveled all around the South in the 1940s. She met new people and saw how Black folks were treated in different towns—some towns were welcoming, and some were not. No matter where she was and who was in the audience, she felt larger-than-life. So, she renamed herself Big Mama Thornton.

After years on the road, Willie moved to Houston, Texas, to record music she hoped would play on the radio. Her first big break came in 1953. Willie's voice came through the speakers on radios everywhere: "You ain't nothin' but a hound dog!" she sang, loud and proud. The record blew up! Elvis Presley liked it so much that he rerecorded a rock version of the song. But Willie would always be the first to have sung such an iconic hit.

Willie went on to make several albums, including a gospel album, inspired by her days listening to her dad preach and her mom sing in a small-town church.

DECEMBER 11, 1926–JULY 25, 1984
UNITED STATES OF AMERICA

"'HOUND DOG' JUST TOOK OFF LIKE A JET."
—BIG MAMA THORNTON

ILLUSTRATION BY
RAFAELA RIJO-NÚÑEZ

BJÖRK

Once there was a girl who grew up exploring the winding trails and rushing rivers of her home in Iceland. She found beautiful melodies in the sounds of nature. Her name was Björk, which in Icelandic means "birch," like the tree. At her music school, she sang and studied piano and flute. When she was 12, Björk released her first album. The record company asked her for a similar-sounding follow-up, but Björk refused. She had more to discover, and like a waterfall tumbling over a rocky cliff, she wouldn't let anyone hold her back.

As a teenager Björk formed bands with friends. She tried out styles from jazz to punk, and put her own spin on them. Then Björk and a group of other musicians were invited to perform on a live radio show. She sang in her high, haunting voice and experimented with howls and shrieks.

The music world took notice.

Fans gravitated toward her unique sound, and Björk's career began to take off. She worked with choirs, harpists, and orchestras to create melodies as rich and distinct as her voice. The music videos she made captured the untamed natural landscape of her home in Iceland. Outside of music, Björk loved fashion. She sought out pieces that were one of a kind. In 2001, she posed on the Oscars red carpet wearing a dress in the shape of a swan, complete with a feathered skirt!

As her success continues, Björk makes herself heard in other ways, too, raising awareness for issues like protecting the environment and women's reproductive rights. Through it all, Björk remains as free as the wind blowing across the fields of Iceland. She dances to her own beat and encourages others to find their rhythm and move to it too.

BORN NOVEMBER 21, 1965
ICELAND

ILLUSTRATION BY
JULIETTE TOMA

"NATURE HAS ALWAYS
BEEN IMPORTANT TO ME.
IT HAS ALWAYS BEEN IN
MY MUSIC."
—BJÖRK

BLACKPINK

K-POP BAND

Once there were four girls who grew up in very different places around the world, from bustling cities to vast farmland, all with dreams of becoming singers. When Jisoo, Jennie, Lisa, and Rosé auditioned for an entertainment company, they each gained three new sisters. The four young musicians were selected to form the K-pop band Blackpink. They met in South Korea and spent years laughing together in the dance studio and belting out lyrics in preparation to make their musical debut.

With their powerful voices, fun fashion choices, and impressive dance moves the four girls captured the world. Their first single, "Boombayah," a bouncy party song, reached number one on the Billboard World Digital Songs chart faster than any song by a K-pop girl group had before.

On their meteoric rise to fame, each of the girls' different strengths came into play. Jennie's focus kept the group on track while Jisoo made sure everyone was feeling their best before each big performance. Main vocalist Rosé thrived in the spotlight, and Lisa's playful energy had the girls smiling even on tough days. Their sweet friendship touched fans far and wide.

In 2019, Blackpink made history again, this time as the first K-pop girl group to perform at the popular American music festival Coachella. Singing, rapping, and dancing their way onstage in eye-catching jeweled outfits, they quickly got the crowd fired up. Fans cheered for them in many different languages.

"Tonight," Rosé told the beaming audience, "I think we've learned so deeply that music brings us [together] as one."

JISOO, BORN JANUARY 3, 1995
JENNIE, BORN JANUARY 16, 1996
LISA, BORN MARCH 27, 1997
ROSÉ, BORN FEBRUARY 11, 1997
SOUTH KOREA, NEW ZEALAND, THAILAND

"EVEN IF WE'RE 70 AND WE HAVE DIFFERENT LIVES, I'LL STILL FEEL LIKE I'M BLACKPINK."
—JENNIE

ILLUSTRATION BY EMMA EUBANKS

DOLLY PARTON

COUNTRY SINGER AND SONGWRITER

SCAN TO HEAR MORE!

Once there was a girl named Dolly who dreamed big dreams and loved singing to her brothers and sisters—all eleven of them! She had no idea that one day, she'd trade her front porch in the Great Smoky Mountains for stages around the world.

Dolly's family struggled. They lived in a one-room cabin with no electricity, but they were rich in other ways, like the music they shared. Wrapped in a coat her mother sewed from rags, Dolly began writing songs while strumming a homemade guitar. She was singing on TV by the time she was 10. After becoming the first person in her family to graduate high school, Dolly headed to Nashville to pursue music.

With her songwriting skills, bright smile, and bold fashion sense, Dolly dazzled country music listeners. She wrote her songs whenever inspiration struck. Once, while riding on a tour bus and thinking about the mountain home she'd left behind, lyrics suddenly came to her. She quickly scribbled them on the only paper she could find—a dry-cleaning receipt! Those lyrics would become "Coat of Many Colors," a sweet song honoring her mother's love for her and that homemade coat that kept her warm as a little girl.

From belting out tunes with her family to performing in front of thousands, Dolly has never forgotten that her dream "was to make as many people happy as I could in this life." So, inspired by her father, who couldn't read or write, Dolly created a program that sends free books to young children to encourage their love of reading. A music legend with a truly generous spirit, Dolly uplifts others however she can.

BORN JANUARY 19, 1946
UNITED STATES OF AMERICA

"FIND OUT WHO YOU ARE, AND DO IT ON PURPOSE."
—DOLLY PARTON

ILLUSTRATION BY JANIE SECKER

ELLA FITZGERALD

JAZZ SINGER

In 1917 on a spring day in Virginia, a jazz legend was born. Before she captivated the world with her singing voice, she was a girl named Ella growing up outside of New York City. Ella played baseball with the neighborhood boys, hooting and hollering as they ran through the streets. She listened to jazzy songs like Mamie Smith's "Crazy Blues," smiling and swinging her hips with friends. Some nights, she'd take the train down to Harlem's Apollo Theater, the birthplace of jazz.

Ella's world grew quiet when her mother died after a car accident. Ella started to skip school and eventually got in trouble with the police. She was sent to a reform school, and when she got out, everything had changed. She saw people in tattered clothes lined up for food at soup kitchens and children with dusty faces begging on the street. It was the middle of the Great Depression, and life was tough. But Ella was tough too.

One night, when she was 17, she made her way back to the Apollo for amateur night—a special night where regular people showed off their talents. The crowd was rowdy, but when she began to sing, they quieted. She sang one of her mother's favorite songs in her smooth, clear voice. When she reached the last note, everyone cheered. *Encore, encore!* they shouted.

"I knew I wanted to sing before people the rest of my life," Ella said, and she did exactly that. Ella became a bandleader and traveled all over the world to perform with jazz greats like Duke Ellington, Nat King Cole, and Frank Sinatra. Over her lifetime, she won 13 Grammy Awards and became known as the First Lady of Song.

APRIL 25, 1917–JUNE 15, 1996

UNITED STATES OF AMERICA

"IT ISN'T WHERE YOU CAME FROM; IT'S WHERE YOU'RE GOING THAT COUNTS."
—ELLA FITZGERALD

ILLUSTRATION BY
KIM HOLT

EVELYN GLENNIE

PERCUSSIONIST

When she was eight years old, Evelyn started to lose her hearing. But she was still determined to learn piano. Music was a treasured part of her life on her family's farm in northern Scotland, and she was afraid of losing the songs that had touched her heart. When she was 12, she started learning percussion instruments too, like drums and the xylophone, though by then she was almost completely deaf.

At school, Evelyn learned to recognize high and low sounds by placing her hands on the walls to feel the vibrations while her teacher played instruments. She opted to remove her hearing aids, and her body became a resonating chamber. She could hear her drums through the thump and thrum she felt deep in her bones. Evelyn found that music could still touch her heart.

By 16, she had earned herself a place at the Royal Academy of Music in London, where she was their first deaf student. But Evelyn never wanted to be seen as a deaf musician. "I'm a musician who happens to be deaf," she says. Evelyn embarked on her lifelong mission to "teach the world to listen" through her work as a solo percussionist and composer. When Evelyn performs, it's impossible not to be transfixed by her focus as she bangs a deep, bold melody on her drums or taps out a delicate tune on the xylophone.

Evelyn has won many awards and teaches young musicians. In 2012, she led a thousand drummers in the Opening Ceremony of the London Olympic Games. She is also the president of Help Musicians, which offers financial aid and other resources to musicians throughout their careers. There's no matching the unique rhythm of Evelyn's life.

BORN JULY 19, 1965

SCOTLAND

"LOSING MY HEARING
MADE ME A BETTER
LISTENER."
EVELYN GLENNIE

FEA

PUNK ROCK BAND

One night in 1994, two best friends named Phanie and Jenn went to a punk rock show, and it changed their lives forever.

As one of the bands came onstage and started playing, the two teenage girls from San Antonio, Texas, were spellbound by what they saw. Babes in Toyland was loud and fearless. Phanie and Jenn looked at each other. They were thinking the same thing: *Let's form a band!* And so they did. In time, they became a trio, with Phanie's little sister, Nina, joining them with a notebook full of lyrics and a powerful set of lungs. They called their band Girl in a Coma.

In 2014, while Nina was taking a break from Girl in a Coma, an exciting, new musical adventure between Jenn and Phanie began. With the *ba-boom ba-boom* of Phanie's drums and the of low strums of Jenn's bass, it was as if no time at all had passed since that special evening 20 years before. They found their vocalist in blue-haired rocker Letty Martinez, and together they began writing energetic punk songs about feminism, strength, and politics.

As proud Chicanas, they write and sing songs in both English and Spanish to send the message that Latina punk music needs to be heard. They called the band Fea, which means "ugly" in Spanish. People were shocked that they would choose that name, but like all great punk rockers, Phanie, Jenn, and Letty do not care what others think or say about them.

Fea plays their music all over the world. They've even gone on tour with their heroes, Babes in Toyland. With younger and younger female fans attending Fea's shows, they have become childhood heroes too.

PHANIE DIAZ, BORN JUNE 8, 1980
JENN ALVA, BORN APRIL 17, 1980
LETTY MARTINEZ, BORN APRIL 2, 1986
UNITED STATES OF AMERICA

ILLUSTRATION BY
YAMILA YJILIOFF

"WE WANTED TO START OUR DREAM
BAND PRETTY MUCH PAY HOMAGE TO
THE RIOT GRRRL MOVEMENT."
—JENN ALVA

IVY QUEEN

RAPPER AND SINGER

Once upon a time, there was a girl from Puerto Rico who dreamed about becoming a queen.

Growing up, Martha helped take care of her younger siblings. When she did have free time, she spent it listening to hip-hop music and scribbling down her own rhymes.

At 18, Martha moved to San Juan, Puerto Rico. It was time for her first rap battle, and the place to go was the Noise. It was a small, sweaty nightclub. People crowded in to dance while rappers battled one another using their skilled rhymes. The cheers from the audience would determine whose lyrics were the best.

When Martha arrived, the beats were booming into the street. She was a little scared as she took hold of the mic, but she was ready. Her male opponent started making fun of her hair. Martha pretended she was a boxer, shrugging off his words and staring him down. Then it was her turn. She took a breath, and launched into her rap, working with the fast beats and the excited energy in the air.

The crowd went wild. Martha finally got her crown. She chose the stage name Ivy Queen, becoming the first woman accepted into the Noise's group of rappers, DJs, and producers. Together, they helped make a new genre of music called reggaeton that grew from popular rhythms found in Spanish reggae, dancehall, and hip-hop. Ivy Queen said it was like reggaeton had special powers because of the way it made people move.

Today, Ivy Queen reigns solo, writing empowering songs and gaining more fans and crowns as the Queen of Reggaeton.

BORN MARCH 4, 1972
PUERTO RICO

ILLUSTRATION BY
CAMILA GRAY

"IN MY 20 YEARS
AS AN ARTIST,
I'VE ALWAYS
REPRESENTED
WOMEN WITH
LYRICS THAT ARE
EMPOWERING."
—IVY QUEEN

JODY GERSON

MUSIC EXECUTIVE

Once there was a girl who grew up among the stars. Every weekend, Jody and her brother attended a matinee show at their father's nightclub. They snuck peeks from behind the velvet curtains backstage as great entertainers of the time like Frank Sinatra crooned into the microphone. They watched as crowds roared and whistled for encores.

"I knew very early on I wasn't going to be a performer," Jody remembers of seeing those shows, "but I was always fascinated by talent."

Jody set goals for herself and studied hard to make them happen. She was the first person in her family to attend college. Later, she worked her way up to a long-term leadership position at a music company, where she signed on artists like Alicia Keys and Norah Jones to record their future albums with her team.

Though Jody never wanted to be in the spotlight herself, being around talent since she was young made it easy for her to recognize that star potential. In 2015, she took over as chairman and CEO of Universal Music Publishing Group. The girl who loved watching performers dazzle a crowd became the first female boss of a multinational music company.

Jody's mission is not to be the only one, however. In between working with some of today's biggest entertainers, like Lady Gaga, Halsey, and Billie Eilish, Jody helped create She Is The Music, a nonprofit dedicated to increasing the number of women working in the music industry.

Sometimes, Jody still goes to shows with her family for fun, remaining as enchanted as she always was by the stars.

BORN 1961
UNITED STATES OF AMERICA

"I FEEL A GREAT RESPONSIBILITY TO DO RIGHT BY OTHER WOMEN."
—JODY GERSON

ILLUSTRATION BY FLAVIA SORRENTINO

JONI MITCHELL

SINGER AND SONGWRITER

SCAN TO HEAR MORE!

As a little girl, Joni looked across the sprawling wheat fields and rusty railroad tracks outside her home and dreamed of seeing the world. "My family could only afford to get me the box of eight Crayola crayons, but I craved the one with all 24 colors. I wanted magenta and turquoise and silver and gold," she once said.

Joni had a big imagination, but she got in trouble during piano lessons for making up her own melodies. Then when she was nine, she contracted polio. In the hospital, she sang to other patients, who applauded her creativity.

When she grew up, music helped Joni through another hardship in her life: giving her daughter up for adoption. Joni had just left art school and couldn't care for her baby. To process her grief, she poured her energy into songwriting.

Joni traveled along the East Coast scribbling down lyrics on trains and buses. She plucked her guitar strings and sang in coffee shops and clubs. Fans related to the stories in her songs. In "The Circle Game," she wrote about a boy growing up and going from catching dragonflies to learning to drive to achieving his dreams. In "Big Yellow Taxi," Joni sang about environmental change, writing the iconic line: "They paved paradise and put up a parking lot."

Soon Joni met other musicians, and her star began to rise. In 1970, her album *Clouds* won a Grammy Award for Best Folk Performance. Joni was just getting started. Over the course of her career, she made folk, pop, and jazz albums and won many more awards. She is known as one of the greatest songwriters ever. And it's all because she was never afraid to use all the colors of her imagination.

BORN NOVEMBER 7, 1943
CANADA AND UNITED STATES OF AMERICA

"I SEE MUSIC AS FLUID
ARCHITECTURE."
—JONI MITCHELL

ILLUSTRATION BY
LIVELY SCOUT

SCAN TO HEAR MORE!

KATHLEEN HANNA

PUNK ROCK SINGER AND SONGWRITER

Kathleen was nine years old when she went to her first feminist rally. She was enthralled by all the loud, proud women gathered in Washington, DC. "It was the first time I had ever been in a big crowd of women yelling," Kathleen said. "And it really made me want to do it forever."

As a teenager, Kathleen started writing and performing slam poetry. Later, she turned to music, gravitating toward the high-energy sound of punk rock. In 1990, Kathleen formed the band Bikini Kill with three talented musicians: guitarist Billy Karren, bassist Kathi Wilcox, and drummer Tobi Vail.

Kathleen used her big voice to spread the message that girls and women are stronger when they work together. Her powerful lyrics, accompanied by fast-stomping drum beats and melodies, were hard to ignore. At concerts, Kathleen would tell the crowd, "Girls to the front!," because girls often got shoved to the back. Kathleen didn't want this to happen to anyone. At Bikini Kill's rollicking shows, women knew they could jump, dance, and rock out safely—with a great view of the band.

Sometimes, Kathleen shared her views through her writing instead of music. In "Riot Grrrl Manifesto," she wrote: "We are angry at a society that tells us Girl = Dumb, Girl = Bad, Girl = Weak." Many people knew Kathleen was a strong and positive force for women, but others were angry at her beliefs. Kathleen kept going. Through art and activism, an entire feminst movement took shape.

Bikini Kill's impact on punk rock is everlasting. They are still getting together to play shows today, 25 years after the band officially broke up. Kathleen has truly kept her promise to make her voice heard forever.

BORN NOVEMBER 12, 1968
UNITED STATES OF AMERICA

ILLUSTRATION BY
TAMIKI

"I'M NOT A
GODDESS . . .
I'M A REGULAR
PERSON WHO
TOOK FEMINISM—
WHICH I HAVE A
DEEP CONNECTION
TO—AND MIXED
IT WITH MUSIC,
WHICH I REALLY
LOVE TO DO."
—KATHLEEN HANNA

LAURA JANE GRACE

PUNK ROCK SINGER, SONGWRITER, AND GUITARIST

One day, in Texas, a four-year-old kid put her hand on the TV screen. Behind the static fuzz was a captivating woman named Madonna dancing confidently. *That's me*, she thought. Even though Laura Jane knew how she felt inside, she'd been told she was a boy since she was born.

Laura Jane felt alone and confused about who she was for many years. There was one thing in her life that made her feel less pain, and that was punk rock. Playing music felt like an armor Laura Jane could put on. Behind a disguise of passionate lyrics and guitar riffs, she could express how she really felt. She called her act Against Me!

Laura Jane's friend Kevin joined Against Me! He didn't own a drum kit, so he would bang on pickle buckets he'd found in a dumpster. It didn't matter because when they were jamming, it was as though they were reading each other's minds. In those moments, Laura Jane felt good.

Over the years, more musicians joined Against Me! Some left, but the band's fame grew, and so did Laura Jane. While she still struggled with her identity, her fans boosted her confidence. In hot and crowded punk venues, she would strum her guitar and sing about wanting to wear dresses and not feeling like a man.

Then Laura Jane woke up one morning in her thirties. The time had come for her to explain how she felt inside. She told her fans she was transgender. Not everyone understood, but many people told her they loved her. The music played on.

BORN NOVEMBER 8, 1980
UNITED STATES OF AMERICA

"PUNK ROCK—
ESPECIALLY DIY PUNK
ROCK—TAUGHT ME
THAT I DON'T NEED
TO ASK PERMISSION
FROM SOMEONE TO
STAND UP AND SAY
WHAT'S ON MY MIND."
—LAURA JANE GRACE

ILLUSTRATION BY
GABY VERDOOREN

LES FILLES DE ILLIGHADAD

FOLK BAND

 nce upon a time, in a small village on the edge of the Sahara desert, a 10-year-old girl taught herself to play guitar. Her name was Fatou.

To get to Fatou's village, Illighadad in Niger, visitors have to take a bumpy drive through tall sand dunes. Life in the scorching African desert is hard sometimes. There's no electricity or running water, but hundreds of families have lived there peacefully with their goats and cattle for centuries. And there is always music.

Whenever a baby is born or a young couple gets married, the people in Fatou's village gather around drums made from stretched goat skin to sing and dance to folk songs. When families argue, they always make peace through the music. Their voices harmonize under the desert sky. At these gatherings, girls always sang. Old rules said only boys could play the guitar. Fatou thought it was time for a change. Her father disapproved, but she did not give up. Instead, she started a band with her cousin in 2016.

They called themselves Les Filles de Illighadad, or the Daughters of Illighadad. With an acoustic guitar, a calabash—a drum made from a type of melon floating in water—and their melodic voices, the women created a special sound.

After they recorded their first album, the band traveled all around the world. In head wraps and flowing dresses, they shared a piece of their village with new fans. Their music serves a bigger purpose though. For Les Filles de Illighadad, making music is a way to buy things like medicine for the people in the beautiful faraway place they call home.

BIRTH DATES UNKNOWN
NIGER

ILLUSTRATION BY
TYLER BARNETT

"IT IS VERY RARE
THAT YOU SEE A
TUAREG WOMAN
PLAYING GUITAR."
—FATOU SEIDI GHALI

LIZZO

POP SINGER, SONGWRITER, AND FLUTIST

There once was a young girl named Melissa who felt most confident when she was playing music. The sounds of her flute melted away the insecurities she had about her body.

When Melissa started a new school at 10 years old, she joined the school band. The band was different than she expected. Instead of playing old classical tunes, she and her bandmates filled their concerts with fun pop songs—the ones they heard on the radio!

Every day after school, Melissa would practice the flute for hours. The sheet music was difficult, and the notes would blur across the page, so she listened to the music over and over until she memorized it by ear. When she was 14, she and her friends formed a music group. Melissa wasn't only a flute player. Using the name Lizzo, she became a rapper and singer too!

In college, she found it harder to juggle music and school. When her dad passed away, Lizzo decided to make a change. Life was short, and she was going to chase her dreams. She decided to drop out of college and pursue music full-time, even if some people said she couldn't because of her weight. She chose to love herself—wearing loud colors and bright makeup.

Lizzo joined different girl groups in her city of Minneapolis, singing in dark bars. And in 2014, she got a big break. The iconic pop star Prince noticed Lizzo's talent and invited her and her bandmate to sing and rap on one of his new songs. She said it was like a fairy tale.

After that, her career took off. Now, she travels the world singing her music (and sometimes playing her flute) to sold-out crowds—reminding her fans that no dream is too big, and every body is just right.

BORN APRIL 27, 1988
UNITED STATES OF AMERICA

ILLUSTRATION BY
MONET ALYSSA

"I DON'T THINK THAT LOVING
YOURSELF IS A CHOICE. I THINK
THAT IT'S A DECISION THAT HAS
TO BE MADE FOR SURVIVAL."
—LIZZO

LYDIA CANAAN

ROCK AND ROLL SINGER AND SONGWRITER

Once there was a young girl named Lydia who grew up in the middle of a violent civil war. As people fled her home country of Lebanon and her city crumbled, Lydia held on to what made her feel safe: music.

But Lydia's parents were very strict, and they would not allow her to sing rock music. *Why sing when there are so many more important things to think about?* they said. So Lydia learned songs in secret. She knew that music could help people feel less alone in difficult times and that maybe she could make a difference in her own way.

When she was a teenager, Lydia joined a heavy metal band. They played loud, fast music with booming drums and long guitar riffs. Young people around the country flocked to see them perform. Lydia's powerful voice reverberated through the packed stadiums she played in. The audience could relate to the frustration she felt about the violence all around them.

When a friend of Lydia's died, she wrote a song called "Why All the Hurt?" that quickly climbed to the top of the charts in Lebanon. Her passionate voice could be heard on radios throughout the country. In the middle of all the war and conflict of the 1980s, Lydia performed at one sold-out concert after another, becoming the first rock star in the Middle East.

Lydia didn't stop there. As she got older, she used her platform to speak out on all kinds of injustice. As a United Nations delegate, she's stood up for many who have been treated unfairly, from people imprisoned for their beliefs to abused animals. Lydia always knew that through music, she could change lives.

BORN DECEMBER 2, 1965
LEBANON

ILLUSTRATION BY
ANSHIKA KHULLAR

"SINCE I COULD
NOT CHANGE THE
WORLD AROUND ME,
I CREATED A WORLD
INSIDE ME."
—LYDIA CANAAN

MERCEDES SOSA

FOLK SINGER

Once upon a time in Argentina, a little girl named Mercedes lived in a house with lots of love but not even a single toy. Across the street was a great, big park where every day, Mercedes and her siblings would go to play games until late into the evening. The buzzing of the cicadas in the trees helped them ignore the rumbling sounds of their hungry bellies.

When Mercedes was 15, her friends and teachers encouraged her to audition for a singing competition. To her surprise, she won. Her songs were played on the radio. A global tour soon followed.

Onstage, Mercedes felt so shy she could not look at her audience. In her low, clear voice, she sang folk songs by Latin Americans, which told stories about pain, poverty, and human rights. Many people loved listening to her sing, but the armed men in power in Argentina believed the songs were dangerous. During one of her concerts, the music suddenly stopped. Men stormed the stage and arrested Mercedes on the spot. Thanks to her supporters, she was released in less than a day and soon performed again. Then, those same powerful men forced Mercedes to leave Argentina.

Homesick in Europe, Mercedes began looking audiences in the eyes to show the world she was not afraid of anyone. When Mercedes returned to Argentina a few years later, she brought with her newfound confidence and international fame. The people welcomed her warmly, and soon after, the cruel military group controlling the country collapsed.

Mercedes never thought she would sing for a living, but she kept singing until she died. In her lifetime, she had recorded more than 70 albums.

JULY 9, 1935–OCTOBER 4, 2009
ARGENTINA

"LIFE CHOSE ME
TO SING."
—MERCEDES SOSA

M.I.A.

RAPPER

SCAN TO HEAR MORE!

Once upon a time, a young Tamil girl named Mathangi lived in Sri Lanka. Old men sold fruit on the street as ladies walked beneath colorful umbrellas to shield them from the sun. Tamils were the minority. Mathangi didn't understand what that meant until she turned 10 and men with large guns appeared on the streets. A civil war had broken out, and Mathangi's father joined the fight for Tamil independence.

Mathangi fled to London with her mom and siblings. As refugees, their family dealt with a lot of racism. Mathangi decided to go by Maya so she wouldn't have to constantly pronounce her name for her new classmates. With her father still fighting in Sri Lanka, Maya wondered how she could make a difference in the world. She decided to study filmmaking in college. But when she graduated, she received a phone call that changed her life.

Her favorite cousin back in Sri Lanka had gone MIA (missing in action) during all the violence, so she went back home to try to find him. When she arrived, it was chaos. The sound of bombs rang out day and night. Maya never found her cousin, but she knew she had to tell the world what was happening.

Renaming herself M.I.A., she started making music. She wrote catchy, meaningful lyrics and rapped to bumping beats. She used her music videos as a way to get important messages across. In the video for "Borders," M.I.A. holds her stare at the camera as refugees behind her try to flee to safety by boat, on foot, and over walls. Some people don't like that her music tackles heavy subjects, and certain things she has said have caused heated debates. But M.I.A. always stays true to herself.

BORN JULY 18, 1975

SRI LANKA AND UNITED KINGDOM

"I WANTED TO MAKE
MUSIC THAT YOU FELT
IN YOUR GUT."
—M.I.A.

ILLUSTRATION BY
MANJIT THAPP

NANDI BUSHELL

DRUMMER

Once there was a little girl who was born with rhythm. In her quiet English town, Nandi gravitated toward music, especially the steady *thump, thump, thump* of a good drum beat. While her parents made dinner, her dad played videos of his favorite musicians, like the Beatles. It was always the drummers that Nandi couldn't take her eyes off. One day, she walked into a toy store with her parents, and there it was waiting for her on the shelves: a drum set! *Pleeease, Mum!* she begged.

It was the start of something epic. With her dad's help, Nandi learned how to play. She practiced every day in the living room. Once she started to get the hang of it, her dad had an idea. Why not jam together at their local pub? On the weekends, Nandi would stay up past her bedtime so she and her dad could try out songs as neighbors munched on fish and chips.

After about a year, Nandi had an idea of her own. She started posting videos online of rocking out on her drum set. Soon Nandi was receiving comments from her favorite musicians, like Lenny Kravitz. TV shows began to reach out to her for interviews. Dave Grohl from the band Foo Fighters even invited her to play onstage at one of their concerts.

Nandi was nervous to play in front of so many people, but once the whine of the electric guitar pierced the air, she was in her element. She twirled a drumstick in one hand, high above her head. Dave began to sing, and Nandi's face broke into a wide smile. Her curly hair bounced as her arms flurried around the drums. It was a dream come true.

BORN APRIL 28, 2010

SOUTH AFRICA AND UNITED KINGDOM

"IT'S NOT ABOUT THE NUMBERS [ON SOCIAL MEDIA]. IT'S ABOUT: PEOPLE LIKE IT, AND THEY FEEL HAPPY WATCHING IT."
—NANDI BUSHELL

ILLUSTRATION BY SHAREE MILLER

NERVO

DJS

Twin sisters Liv and Mim's music dreams began in the audience at dance-until-you-drop music festivals. As they moved to the music, their teenage hearts beat to the thrilling rhythms of electronic dance music. "Purple hair and purple lipstick; we did it all," Mim said of their festival-going days.

At home, the sisters wrote songs in their bedroom, hoping they would be on those festival stages one day. Their talent and passion for music earned them spots at their country's prestigious Opera Australia Academy. But Liv and Mim had their sights set on a career in pop music. And they always knew they were stronger together. "Working together was a natural move for us as we have similar tastes, love to be together, and are each other's biggest supporters," they have said.

When they were just 18, Liv and Mim got the attention of a major music publisher. They began writing hits for musicians like Kesha, Miley Cyrus, David Guetta, and more. After their song "When Love Takes Over" won a Grammy, they decided they needed new challenges, like writing music they would perform themselves and sharpening their DJ skills. They spun records in nightclubs and on stages all over the world to make their dream a reality. Soon they were performing at the kinds of shows they had enjoyed since they were teenagers. At Tomorrowland, a festival in Belgium, the sisters kept the party going all night with their bumping beats and bouncy energy.

Together as Nervo, they now headline their own tours and are regularly featured in fashion magazines across the globe, making their bold and upbeat style as recognizable as their music. Whatever they dream up next, there's nothing this duo can't do.

BORN FEBRUARY 18, 1982
AUSTRALIA

"LET'S FACE IT, YOU CAN BE CREATIVE IN MANY WAYS. FROM WEARING CRAZY CLOTHES AND GREAT MAKEUP TO PLAYING INSANE TUNES. IT'S ALL GOOD."
—MIM NERVO

ILLUSTRATION BY DOROTA JANICKA

OLIVIA RODRIGO

POP SINGER AND SONGWRITER

Once there was a girl who longed for others to see themselves in the songs she wrote. Olivia didn't have a lot of the experiences many girls share growing up. She was homeschooled, she was best friends with her parents, and she was the star of two shows on Disney Channel. Olivia listened to the songs of artists she admired and hoped to write lyrics that would make other people feel seen too. Then she had her heart broken for the first time. Suddenly words anyone could relate to poured out of her as she played her guitar.

Olivia's single "Drivers License" went viral, shattering records for daily plays around the world. Suddenly girls everywhere were belting out Olivia's lyrics, in their cars, with their friends, and from the audience when she performed for them.

Some critics gave Olivia a hard time for writing so many songs about heartbreak. She refused to let their comments get to her. "I'm a teenage girl, I write about stuff that I feel really intensely—and I feel heartbreak and longing really intensely—and I think that's authentic and natural," she said.

Olivia won three Grammy Awards for her debut album, *Sour*, and she isn't stopping there. She also uses her platform to take a stand on issues that matter to her, like denouncing the US Supreme Court justices who voted against women's reproductive rights. She even dedicated a song—full of angry feelings—to them onstage.

She may have grown up differently than most girls, but the emotions in Olivia's songs are felt by people everywhere.

BORN FEBRUARY 20, 2003
UNITED STATES OF AMERICA

ILLUSTRATION BY
VIVI CAMPOS

"IT'S SO EXCITING TO
ME TO WATCH YOUNG
WOMEN'S VOICES BE HEARD
AND APPRECIATED AND
CELEBRATED. . ."
—OLIVIA RODRIGO

QUEEN LATIFAH

RAPPER

Once upon a time in Newark, New Jersey, there was a girl named Dana who had big dreams and a big personality to match. Growing up, Dana played basketball and went to church with her family. *Dana, you're taller than the boys!* her best friend, Shakim, would tease. But Dana didn't care. She was comfortable standing out.

One day at school, Dana picked up a book of Arabic names from a shelf. She flipped through the pages until she landed on Latifah, which meant "delicate, sensitive, and kind." She tucked the name away in her memory, somehow knowing it would come in handy.

By the time she was in high school, Dana was playing varsity basketball. *You can call me the Queen,* she'd say. Basketball wasn't the only thing that made her feel powerful, though. Dana's interest in performing was growing. She joined an all-female rap group and began recording her own songs. At 19, she released her first album, *All Hail the Queen*. Remembering the name she'd come across years ago, she called herself Queen Latifah.

Her songs played on radios all around the United States. In "Ladies First," she rapped about women following their dreams. "Who said the ladies couldn't make it, you must be blind," she rapped over a catchy beat. All her life, Queen Latifah had demanded respect, and she wasn't going to stop now.

Queen Latifah quickly became one of rap's top artists, and she won a Grammy for Best Rap Solo Performance in 1995. She has also made award-winning movies, starred in TV shows, and hosted her own talk show. There's never been any stopping this queen of big dreams.

BORN MARCH 18, 1970
UNITED STATES OF AMERICA

"FAILURE IS A PART OF SUCCESS."
—QUEEN LATIFAH

ILLUSTRATION BY
TAINA CUNION

RONNIE SPECTOR

ROCK AND ROLL SINGER

Once upon a time, there was a girl named Veronica who everyone called Ronnie. Ronnie grew up in Spanish Harlem in New York City. She ran around her neighborhood with her sister, Estelle, and her cousin Nedra. The three were inseparable.

Their days were filled with music. Hearing songs drifting out into the street from open apartment windows on a Friday night was one of Ronnie's favorite things. At family gatherings, Ronnie, Estelle, and Nedra would sing together. They'd get close, and everyone would grow quiet as Estelle counted them off, snapping her fingers before they harmonized.

When they were teenagers, the girls formed a group called the Darling Sisters. During the day, Estelle worked behind the shiny glass beauty counter at Macy's, where she scoped out the newest fashion for the Darling Sisters' next gig. Whether they wore form-fitting bedazzled dresses or pastel suits with handmade buttons, the trio was always perfectly coordinated. On Saturday nights, the girls would take the train to the Peppermint Lounge to perform. Women with big hair and men in slick suits tried a new dance called the Twist as the girls crooned onstage. One night, a DJ called Murray the K saw them sing and hired them on the spot.

In 1963, Ronnie took center stage as the lead singer of the group, and the trio became the Ronettes. It wasn't long before they were making hits, like "Be My Baby," which skyrocketed on the charts. As Ronnie got older, she had some tough times. With the help of her family, she had to escape an unhappy marriage. In a book about her life, Ronnie wrote about the good times and the bad—and how music always got her through.

AUGUST 10, 1943–JANUARY 12, 2022
UNITED STATES OF AMERICA

"WE DIDN'T DO IT FOR THE MONEY . . . ALL WE WANTED TO DO WAS ROCK 'N' ROLL, TO HAVE FUN, AND WE DID."
—RONNIE SPECTOR

ILLUSTRATION BY KELSEE THOMAS

SELENA QUINTANILLA PÉREZ

TEJANO SINGER

From the time she was a little girl, Selena's rich, smooth singing voice moved everyone who listened.

Selena was nine when she and her siblings formed a band. They were called Selena y Los Dinos. Selena became the lead singer, and her older brother and sister played bass guitar and drums. They practiced every day and began playing to small audiences in their home state of Texas.

Life was tough for Selena's family. They lost their home, and Selena y Los Dinos was making little money. Their luck changed when the band started playing Tejano, a popular style of Mexican American music bursting with emotion and brisk rhythms. Some people thought Selena shouldn't be singing Tejano music since it was usually sung by men. She didn't let that stop her. Eventually, Selena went solo, and her career skyrocketed.

Her concerts began drawing crowds of thousands. In 1995, Selena performed at the Houston Astrodome to an audience of 61,000 people. She arrived at the show on a white horse-drawn carriage and took to the stage in a sparkly purple jumpsuit. Her smile spread from ear to ear as she looked out at the crowd. "Manos arriba!" Selena shouted as the music began. The crowd lifted their hands in the air, dancing and singing along with her. Sadly, this spectacular evening would be Selena's last performance.

"If you have a dream," Selena once said, "don't let anyone take it away." Many of Selena's own dreams were realized but not all of them. Tragically, Selena lost her life at 23. Her music and journey to stardom will never be forgotten.

APRIL 16, 1971–MARCH 31, 1995
UNITED STATES OF AMERICA

ILLUSTRATION BY
EUGENIA MELLO

"I WANT TO BE
REMEMBERED
NOT ONLY AS AN
ENTERTAINER, BUT
AS A PERSON WHO
CARED A LOT, AND
I GAVE THE BEST
THAT I COULD."
—SELENA
QUINTANILLA PÉREZ

TIA FULLER

SAXOPHONIST

When Tia was little, she wanted to be just like her big sister, Shamie. At home, Tia would listen intently as Shamie played the piano. Tia dreamed of playing music, too, and when she was 11, something magical happened. Tia picked up a saxophone for the first time and fell in love.

As she grew up, Tia played all kinds of instruments with her family and in her school's concert, jazz, and marching bands. She studied music at Spelman College, and then, at 26, Tia moved to New York City to pursue a career as a saxophonist. The big city was lonely at times. Often, she was the only woman playing in jazz groups, but she never lost faith.

One day, Tia heard that Beyoncé was looking for musicians for her band. Tia jumped at the chance to audition. Thousands of other female musicians were vying for 10 spots, but Tia made it through round after round. By the third audition, only 60 women were left. In a practice room, Beyoncé and her team hand-selected the musicians who could seamlessly perform rigorous dance moves while playing their instruments. And then, finally, Tia received the news of a lifetime: She was going to be in Beyoncé's band. She was thrilled. "It was Father's Day," Tia said, "and I remember calling my dad and saying, 'Happy Father's Day. I made it!'"

Later, Tia became the second female solo artist ever to recieve a Grammy nomination for Best Instrumental Jazz Album. She also played the music behind the character Dorothea Williams in Pixar's animated movie *Soul*. Today, Tia inspires young musicians as a composer, bandleader, performer, recording artist, and professor at Berklee College of Music.

BORN MARCH 27, 1976
UNITED STATES OF AMERICA

"MAKE DELIBERATE STEPS
TOWARDS YOUR GOAL."
—TIA FULLER

ILLUSTRATION BY
ADRIANA BELLET

WONDAGURL

MUSIC PRODUCER

It's a bird, it's a plane, it's WondaGurl! This superhero story started when a shy girl named Ebony received her first keyboard. She spent hours tapping the keys, learning how to make melodies.

While everyone else was having sleepovers and birthday parties, Ebony made music. She got a drum pad to add rhythmic beats on top of the smooth sound of the keys. She studied the work of famous producers like Timbaland and Hit-Boy. Ebony gave herself a stage name too: WondaGurl— fitting for a girl with musical superpowers.

After a few years of practice, WondaGurl took her music to a beat battle where producers duke it out to see who can make the most creative beats. The first year WondaGurl entered, she didn't perform as well as she hoped. In 2012, she went again.

Onstage under bright purple lights, WondaGurl started playing her tracks. The audience easily found the rhythm and moved to the music. As her beats played, she held her head high, but when the judges were deliberating, nerves took over. Her mom reminded her that if she really wanted this, she needed to face her fears.

She took deep breaths as the judges made the announcement. *And the winner is . . . WondaGurl!* She couldn't stop smiling.

She has produced for Travis Scott, Drake, and Rihanna. She also mentors other young producers. With every success, WondaGurl becomes more and more confident. "The more I grow, and the more I'm in this industry, I feel a lot better and I just feel a lot more comfortable within myself," she says, which of course is another kind of superpower.

BORN DECEMBER 28, 1996
CANADA

54

"IT ALL DEPENDS
ON WHAT YOUR
CHARACTER IS AT
THE END OF THE DAY."
—WONDAGURL

WRITE YOUR STORY

DRAW YOUR PORTRAIT

MEET MORE REBELS

ANGÈLE

In her sleepy Belgian town, Angèle learned to sing and play the piano to keep from being bored. Now, she's one of Europe's biggest and youngest pop stars.

Illustration by Olivia Waller

ARETHA FRANKLIN

Once upon a time, there was a girl who started singing in her father's church. Aretha went on to earn the nickname the Queen of Soul and win 18 Grammy Awards.

Illustration by Johnalynn Holland

BEYONCÉ

One of the most influential pop stars in the world, Beyoncé delights fans with her music, videos, and performances.

Illustration by Eline Van Dam

BILLIE EILISH

When Billie's song "Ocean Eyes" went viral overnight, she went from making music with her big brother at home to touring the globe as a pop star.

Illustration by Paula Zorite

CARMEN MIRANDA

With a colorful look all her own, Carmen Miranda was a popular singer, dancer, and actor.

Illustration by Sonia Lazo

CELIA CRUZ

Once upon a time, a girl named Celia sang her siblings to sleep. She eventually became the Queen of Salsa.

Illustration by Ping Zhu

CLARA ROCKMORE

Clara was an amazing violinist until pain in her arm prevented her from playing. She discovered a new electronic instrument called the theremin, making her a pioneer of electronic music.

Illustration by Cristina Spanò

FRIEDA BELINFANTE

Once upon a time, a girl named Frieda grew up playing the cello and dreaming of having a career in music like her dad did. She grew up to become a renowned music teacher and the first woman conductor of a chamber orchestra in Europe.

Illustration by Gosia Herba

GLORIA ESTEFAN

Born in Cuba, Gloria and her family immigrated to the US when she was very young. With songs in both English and Spanish, she is one of the best-selling Latina musicians of all time.

Illustration by Nan Lawson

HAZEL SCOTT

There once was a girl named Hazel who could play piano perfectly. She was accepted into the famous Juilliard School at just eight years old. Usually they don't accept students until they are 16!

Illustration by Sabrena Khadija

INSOONI

Once there was a girl who was made fun of for looking different than her classmates. She focused on her singing voice instead of their mean words. As an R&B singer, she recorded 19 albums and performed at the Olympics!

Illustration by Taylor McManus

JANIS JOPLIN

Once there was a girl who never felt like she fit in growing up. When she discovered music, everything changed. She went on to become a famous rock and roller known for her powerful voice and high-energy performances.

Illustration by Agata Nowicka

JOJO SIWA

After gaining fans on a popular dance reality show, JoJo's talent combined with her kind and bubbly personality catapulted her to pop-star status.

Illustration by Juliette Toma

KOFFEE

When she was growing up in Jamaica, Koffee started writing and performing her own reggae songs. One of them blew up online! Koffee was the first woman and the youngest person ever to win a Grammy for Best Reggae Album.

Illustration by Monet Alyssa

LADY GAGA

Lady Gaga used music to help her through tough times as a kid. She grew up to be a pop icon, actor, and fierce mental health advocate.

Illustration by Sarah Madden

MADONNA

Madonna always knew she was destined for great things. When she arrived in New York City with only $35 in her pocket, she worked hard and eventually became the world-famous performer she is today.

Illustration by Eline Van Dam

MARIA CALLAS

Once upon a time in Greece, a little girl discovered she had a powerful voice. Maria studied opera singing. She performed around the world and is considered by many to be the most famous soprano ever.

Illustration by Marta Signori

MC SOFFIA

When Soffia was bullied for her dark skin, her mom encouraged her to embrace her heritage. She took her to a hip-hop class, and soon Soffia was writing lyrics and recording in a studio. Her songs were about being proud of who she was and what she looked like.

Illustration by Keisha Okafor

MIRIAM MAKEBA

Miriam used her music to bring attention to the suffering caused by the cruel system of racial segregation known as apartheid. People called her Mama Africa.

Illustration by Helena Morais Soares

NINA SIMONE

Nina wanted Black people to be proud and free. An acclaimed jazz singer, she poured her passion into music.

Illustration by T. S. Abe

POLY STYRENE

Once there was a creative girl named Marianne. Her talent and ambition led her to take the British punk rock scene by storm with a unique look and sound.

Illustration by Kylie Akia Erwin

RENATA FLORES

Renata sings in the Indigenous language Quechua to help perserve the language and the traditions of her ancestors.

Illustration by Tamiki

RIHANNA

Rihanna rose to stardom as a singer. A talented entrepreneur, too, she also created her own fashion and beauty lines.

Illustration by Jestenia Southerland

ROSETTA THARPE

Rosetta learned to play the guitar at just four years old. She was a soul music superstar and a pioneer of rock and roll.

Illustration by Aisha Akeju

TAYLOR SWIFT

As one of the most powerful artists in the music business, Taylor is always reinventing herself. She has released chart-topping country, pop, and folk albums.

Illustration by Anna Dixon

TEMILAYO ABODUNRIN

Once upon a time in Nigeria, a girl discovered the saxophone. She played in church and at weddings. Then she started writing her own songs and taking the stage with big-name jazz artists—all before she turned 12!

Illustration by Rafaela Rijo-Núñez

THE LINDA LINDAS

When a boy at school said something cruel, Eloise, Lucia, Bela, and Mila channeled their anger into a song. Now, they're a punk rock band touring around the country.

Illustration by Janice Chang

VIOLETA PARRA

Violeta fell in love with folk music as a girl. When she grew up, she traveled around her home country of Chile gathering songs, stories, and memories from the people she met.

Illustration by Paola Rollo

XIAN ZHANG

When Xian was little, her father built her a piano. She dreamed of being a concert pianist, but her teacher encouraged her to pursue conducting. She conducted an orchestra for an opera when she was just 20 years old. Now, she is one of the most renowned conductors in the world.

Illustration by Ping Zhu

MAKE YOUR OWN MUSIC!

It's your turn to jam! These activities were designed by Gibson, a company that makes top-tier guitars and other musical intruments.

WRITE YOUR OWN LYRICS

Songwriters like Joni Mitchell and Olivia Rodrigo draw from things that happen in their own lives to write lyrics. They might write about falling in love, moving to a new city, or making a great friend. The stories and themes in songs change, but lyrics often follow a structure like this one:

- **VERSE:** This is the part of the song that tells the story. Verses are typically the longest parts of the songs and they rarely repeat the same words.
- **CHORUS:** A chorus is the part of a song that repeats, which is why these lyrics should be the catchiest!
- **VERSE:** The next verse continues the story of your song with different words than the first verse.
- **CHORUS:** The catchy chorus repeats.
- **BRIDGE:** The bridge changes things up. It's usually just one or two lines and sounds a bit different than the rest of the song. It might speed up the tempo or slow it down.
- **CHORUS:** The song ends with that chorus that listeners love to sing along with.

Using the melody of a song you love, rewrite the lyrics to fit your own life. Maybe it's a lullaby for your dog or an anthem about your best friend. Bonus points: sing it loud and proud for the person (or animal!) you wrote it for.

MAKE A MOOD BOARD

One of the big reasons that a favorite song sticks with you is because of the feelings or memories it conjures in your mind. Pick a song that makes you feel a certain way. It could make you happy, sad, excited, nostalgic, relaxed—whatever! Then grab some paper, markers or crayons, stickers, and old magazines or newspapers. Cut out words and pictures from the magazines and newspapers and arrange them on your paper, then glue them down. This is called a collage. You can also add pictures from your own life or draw or write on parts of the paper with words or doodles that fit with what you're feeling when you listen to the song you picked.

MARCH TO THE BEAT OF YOUR OWN DRUM

Nandi Bushell was always fascinated by the drums. Before she started playing with famous musicians like Dave Grohl, she jammed out with her dad in their living room! You don't need a professional drum set to get started learning how to keep rhythm. Here's how to make your very own drum with regular household items:

1. Grab a coffee tin and some construction paper. Using the coffee label on the tin as a guide, cut the construction paper to fit around the tin. Glue the construction paper to the tin.

2. Next, grab a scrap piece of fabric, like an old T-shirt, or a paper towel and cut a circle that will fit around the top of the coffee tin. Glue it to the top or secure it around the top using a rubber band.

3. Put the plastic lid back on your coffee tin over the fabric.

4. Decorate your drum with stickers, construction paper shapes, or your own doodles.

5. Find some wooden sticks like chopsticks or pencils to use as drumsticks. Put on a song you like and play along. You can keep the beat or make up your own rhythm and rock out!

MAKE A MOOD-BOOSTING PLAYLIST

Dolly Parton has wise words about getting through life's challenges: "The way I see it," she says, "if you want the rainbow, you gotta put up with the rain!" Everyone has days when it feels like that rainbow is never going to show up, but music can help us get out of those bad moods. If you are ever feeling worried—about an upcoming math test or your first day on a new sports team—you can use music to banish your blues. Brainstorm some songs that always put a smile on your face. Grab your grown-up and make a playlist of all those songs on whatever music-streaming service you use. On the morning of that math test, or just before your first big game, hit play for a guaranteed boost.

GUESS THE INSTRUMENT

You read about different instruments in this book, from Lizzo's flute to Evelyn Glennie's xylophone. Now it's time to see if you can identify the distinct sounds instruments make. With your grown-up, look up online and listen to the sounds of a few different instruments, like a saxophone, a trumpet, and a clarinet. Pay close attention to the sounds these instruments make. Then, play a jazz song and call out the different instruments as you hear them. You can even make this a game—see who can name each instrument the fastest!

COMPOSE YOUR OWN MELODY

Music notes are kind of like a special code. They tell the musician which note to play and which key to hit. Reading music takes time to learn, but you can practice composing melodies using your own special code at home. Grab a friend, sibling, or grown-up and follow the steps below.

1. Find a piece of paper and a pencil.
2. Draw a star, a heart, a circle, and a triangle on the top of your paper.
3. Underneath each shape write out a sound that will correspond to it. For instance:
    - Star = one clap
    - Heart = foot stomp
    - Circle = tap a table
    - Triangle = snap your fingers
4. Arrange the symbols in various patterns (for example: a star, a heart, two stars, a circle, a triangle) and give them to your friend to test out. Then, switch roles so they're the composer and you're the musician.

ABOUT GIBSON

Gibson, the leading iconic guitar brand, has shaped the sounds of generations of musicians and music lovers across genres for 128 years. Founded in 1894 and headquartered in Nashville, Gibson Brands has a legacy of world-class craftsmanship, legendary music partnerships, and progressive product evolution that is unrivaled among musical instrument companies. The Gibson Brands portfolio includes Gibson, the leading guitar brand, as well as many of the most beloved and recognizable music brands, including Epiphone, which has been on every stage since 1873; Kramer, the original Made to Rock Hard guitar brand; MESA/Boogie, the home of tone; KRK, behind great music for over 30 years; and Maestro, the founder of effect pedals. Gibson Brands is dedicated to quality, innovation, and sound excellence so music lovers for generations to come will continue to experience music shaped by Gibson Brands. Learn more at Gibson.com and follow them on Twitter, Facebook, Gibson TV, and Instagram.

MORE STORIES!

For more stories about amazing women and girls, check out other Rebel Girls books.

LISTEN TO MORE EMPOWERING STORIES ON THE REBEL GIRLS APP!

Download the app to listen to beloved Rebel Girls stories, as well as brand-new tales of extraordinary women. Filled with the adventures and accomplishments of women from around the world and throughout history, the Rebel Girls app is designed to entertain, inspire, and build confidence in listeners everywhere.

THE ILLUSTRATORS

Twenty-five extraordinary female and nonbinary artists from all over the world illustrated the portraits in this book. Here are their names.

ADRIANA BELLET, **SWEDEN**, 53

ALESSANDRA BERENATO, **ITALY**, 17

ANSHIKA KHULLAR, **UK**, 35

CAMILA GRAY, **BRAZIL**, 21

CAMILLA RU, **UK**, 55

DOROTA JANICKA, **POLAND**, 43

EMMA EUBANKS, **USA**, 11

EUGENIA MELLO, **USA**, 51

FLAVIA SORRENTINO, **ITALY**, 23

GABY VERDOOREN, **USA**, 29

ILIANA GALVEZ, **USA**, 37

JANIE SECKER, **NEW ZEALAND**, 13

JULIETTE TOMA, **USA**, 9

KELSEE THOMAS, **USA**, 49

KIM HOLT, **USA**, 15

LIVELY SCOUT, **AUSTRALIA**, 25

MANJIT THAPP, **UK**, 39

MONET ALYSSA, **USA**, 33

RAFAELA RIJO-NÚÑEZ, **GERMANY**, 7

SHAREE MILLER, **USA**, 41

TAINA CUNION, **USA**, 47

TAMIKI, **PERU**, 27

TYLER BARNETT, **USA**, 31

VIVI CAMPOS, **BRAZIL**, 45

YAMILA YJILIOFF, **ARGENTINA**, 19

ABOUT REBEL GIRLS

REBEL GIRLS is a global, multi-platform empowerment brand dedicated to helping raise the most inspired and confident generation of girls through content, experiences, products, and community. Originating from an international best-selling children's book, Rebel Girls amplifies stories of real-life women throughout history, geography, and field of excellence. With a growing community of nearly 20 million self-identified Rebel Girls spanning more than 100 countries, the brand engages with Generation Alpha through its book series, award-winning podcast, events, and merchandise. With the 2021 launch of the Rebel Girls app, the company has created a flagship destination for girls to explore a wondrous world filled with inspiring true stories of extraordinary women.

As a B corp, we're part of a global community of businesses that meets high standards of social and environmental impact.

Join the Rebel Girls community:
- Facebook: facebook.com/rebelgirls
- Instagram: @rebelgirls
- Twitter: @rebelgirlsbook
- TikTok: @rebelgirlsbook
- Web: rebelgirls.com
- Podcast: rebelgirls.com/podcast
- App: rebelgirls.com/audio

If you liked this book, please take a moment to review it wherever you prefer!